Practical Guide

1. Introduction

Introduction to Short-Term Rentals and Vacation Homes

What is Short-Term Rental

Short-term rental refers to the leasing of properties for limited periods, typically less than 30 days. This type of rental is especially popular among travelers seeking temporary accommodation for vacations, business trips, or brief stays in different cities. Short-term rentals offer flexibility that long-term leases cannot, allowing property owners to maximize their property's yield and renters to enjoy a greater variety of lodging options.

Advantages of Short-Term Rental

1. **Flexibility**: Short-term rentals allow owners to manage their property with greater

How to Start a Short-Term Rental and Vacation Home Business Without Owning Properties

Practical Guide on How to Optimize Short-Term Rental Management and Earn Well

G. Dellis

Copyright © 2024

freedom, renting it out only when they wish and for limited periods.

2. **Profitability**: Owners can often achieve higher returns compared to long-term rentals due to higher daily rates.

3. **Diversification**: Short-term rentals attract a diverse clientele, from tourists to business professionals, increasing occupancy potential.

4. **Fewer Constraints**: Without long-term contracts, owners can decide to use the property for themselves or their families when needed.

Regulations and Legal Requirements

Regulations for short-term rentals can vary significantly from one country to another and even within different cities. It is essential for owners to be aware of local laws to avoid fines or penalties. Some municipalities require specific licenses or the payment of tourist taxes. For example, in Italy, short-term rentals are regulated by laws that mandate contract registration and the payment of a flat tax on rental income.

Managing Short-Term Rentals

Managing a short-term rental requires attention to detail and good organization. Here are some key aspects to consider:

1. **Property Preparation**: The property must be furnished and equipped with all necessary comforts to ensure a pleasant stay. This includes furniture, appliances, linens, and toiletries.

2. **Advertising and Promotion**: It is important to promote the property on online rental platforms such as Airbnb, Booking.com, and Vrbo, providing accurate descriptions and high-quality photos.

3. **Booking Management**: Responding promptly to customer inquiries and managing bookings efficiently is crucial for maintaining a high occupancy rate.

4. **Guest Reception and Support**: Providing a warm welcome and assistance during the stay can make a significant difference in reviews and guest satisfaction.

5. **Cleaning and Maintenance**: Ensuring that the property is always clean and in good condition is essential for attracting and retaining guests.

Vacation Homes

Vacation homes represent a subcategory of short-term rentals, specifically intended for those seeking temporary accommodation for their vacations. These properties can range from small city apartments to large villas in the countryside or by the sea.

Types of Vacation Homes

1. **City Apartments**: Ideal for those wanting to visit cultural or major cities, offering convenience and proximity to main

tourist attractions.

2. **Beach Houses**: Perfect for summer vacations, these properties offer direct or close access to beaches, often with panoramic sea views.

3. **Country Villas**: For those seeking tranquility and relaxation, country villas offer spacious areas, gardens, and often private pools.

4. **Mountain Chalets**: Ideal for winter holidays, offering access to ski slopes and breathtaking mountain views.

Advantages of Vacation Homes

1. **Space and Privacy**: Vacation homes offer more space compared to hotel rooms, allowing travelers to feel at home.

2. **Equipped Kitchen**: Having a kitchen allows savings on meals and the ability to prepare food according to personal preferences.

3. **Authentic Experience**: Staying in a

vacation home allows travelers to live like locals, discovering local habits and traditions.

4. **Flexibility**: Vacation homes offer greater flexibility in check-in and check-out times, better adapting to travelers' needs.

Considerations for Vacation Home Owners

1. **Location**: The property's location is crucial for attracting guests. Properties near tourist attractions, beaches, or city centers are generally more in demand.

2. **Furnishing and Comfort**: Cozy and comfortable furnishings, along with additional amenities like Wi-Fi, air conditioning, and satellite TV, can significantly enhance the property's appeal.

3. **Review Management**: Positive reviews are critical for the success of a vacation home. Providing excellent service and responding promptly to guest feedback can make a difference.

4. **Competitive Rates**: Setting competitive rates, considering seasonality and competitors' prices, is important.

Short-Term Rental and Vacation Home Platforms

Numerous online platforms facilitate the meeting between demand and supply for short-term rentals and vacation homes. Some of the most popular include:

1. **Airbnb**: Probably the most well-known platform, offering a wide range of accommodations worldwide, from private rooms to entire apartments.

2. **Booking.com**: Originally specialized in hotels, now also offers a wide selection of vacation homes and apartments.

3. **Vrbo (Vacation Rentals by Owner)**: Exclusively focused on vacation homes, it is a popular choice for those looking for family or group holiday accommodations.

4. **HomeAway**: Part of the same group as Vrbo, offering a wide range of vacation homes worldwide.

5. **TripAdvisor Rentals**: Part of the famous travel review site, offering a platform for renting vacation homes with the addition of user reviews.

Marketing and Promotion of Vacation Homes

To attract guests and maximize bookings, it is essential to adopt effective marketing strategies. Here are some suggestions:

1. **Professional Photography**: High-quality images are crucial for making a good impression on potential guests.

2. **Detailed Descriptions**: Provide accurate and detailed descriptions of the property, including information on amenities, location, and nearby attractions.

3. **Search Engine Optimization (SEO)**:

Use relevant keywords in descriptions and titles of listings to improve visibility on search engines.

4. **Social Media**: Promoting the property on social media can increase visibility and attract more guests.

5. **Loyalty Programs and Special Offers**: Offering discounts for extended stays, seasonal promotions, and loyalty programs can incentivize repeat bookings.

Local Experiences and Additional Offers

Many travelers seek not just a place to sleep but also unique and authentic experiences. Offering packages that include local activities can be a significant added value. For example:

1. **Food Tours**: Organize tastings of local products or visits to wineries and restaurants.

2. **Outdoor Activities**: Offer experiences like hiking, boat trips, or surfing lessons.

3. **Courses and Workshops**: Propose cooking classes, yoga lessons, or local crafts workshops.

4. **Personalized Services**: Offer additional services like private chefs, babysitters, or tour guides.

Challenges and Solutions in Short-Term Rentals and Vacation Homes

Managing short-term rentals and vacation homes can present various challenges. Here are some of the most common and how to address them:

1. **Competition**: With the growing popularity of short-term rentals, competition has become fierce. Differentiating yourself by offering excellent service and added value can make a difference.

2. **Negative Reviews**: Handle negative reviews professionally, responding promptly and resolving issues raised by guests.

3. **Evolving Regulations**: Stay updated on local regulations and promptly adapt to legislative changes.

4. **Time Management**: Managing multiple bookings can be challenging. Using property management software can simplify the process.

Short-term rentals and vacation homes represent a versatile and profitable solution for both property owners and travelers. They offer flexibility, comfort, and an authentic experience, making them an increasingly popular choice in the tourism sector. However, to succeed in this competitive market, it is essential to pay attention to detail, provide excellent service, and stay updated on local regulations and market trends. With the right strategy, short-term rentals can become a significant source of income and an opportunity to offer memorable experiences to guests.

2. How to Earn with Short-Term Rentals Without Owning Property

The short-term rental market has grown significantly over time, thanks in part to the proliferation of online platforms like Airbnb, Booking.com, and Vrbo. Many believe that entering this market requires property ownership, but there are strategies to earn from short-term rentals without owning properties. These strategies include managing properties for other owners, legal subletting, co-hosting, and utilizing innovative business models.

1. Managing Properties for Others

One of the most common strategies to earn from short-term rentals without owning property is to offer management services for other property owners. This role, often referred to as a property manager, involves handling the daily management of short-term rental properties on behalf of the owners.

a. Services Offered

1. **Booking Management**: Responding to guest inquiries, managing bookings, and keeping the calendar up to date.

2. **Check-in/Check-out**: Welcoming guests upon arrival, providing keys and information about the property, and ensuring a smooth check-out process.

3. **Cleaning and Maintenance**: Coordinating cleaning services between stays and arranging necessary maintenance.

4. **Marketing and Promotion**: Creating and managing listings on short-term rental platforms, optimizing descriptions and photos to attract more bookings.

b. How to Get Started

1. **Create a Service Portfolio**: Clearly define the services offered and establish a

competitive price list.

2. **Networking**: Attend local real estate events, use social media, and network with property owners.

3. **Online Platforms**: Sign up on platforms that connect property managers with property owners, such as Guesty or Vacasa.

4. **Reputation and Reviews**: Build a good reputation through positive reviews from owners and guests.

2. Legal Subletting

Legal subletting, or rental arbitrage, involves renting a property long-term and then subletting it short-term. This model requires obtaining the owner's permission to sublet the property and complying with local laws.

a. Steps to Follow

1. **Market Research**: Analyze the local market to identify areas with high demand for short-term rentals and assess potential earnings.

2. **Finding Willing Owners**: Find owners willing to grant permission for subletting. This may include negotiating favorable terms for both parties.

3. **Contracts and Legality**: Draft clear contracts that include subletting clauses and ensure that subletting is legal in the relevant jurisdiction.

4. **Property Management**: Manage the property as described in the property management section, ensuring maximum occupancy and guest satisfaction.

b. Advantages and Challenges

Advantages:

1. **Low Initial Investment**: No need to purchase property, significantly reducing the initial investment.

2. **Control over Profits**: Ability to set competitive rates and maximize earnings with efficient management.

Challenges:

1. **Permissions and Regulations**: Obtaining the owner's permission and complying with local laws can be complex.

2. **Financial Risk**: Covering the monthly rent even during low occupancy periods.

3. Co-Hosting

Co-hosting involves collaborating with property owners to jointly manage their properties. In this model, the co-host handles part of the management (such as check-in/check-out or maintenance), while the owner manages other activities.

a. How It Works

1. **Task Division**: Clearly define the tasks and responsibilities of each party. For example, the co-host may handle guest communication, while the owner takes care of maintenance.

2. **Profit Sharing**: Establish a profit percentage for the co-host based on the tasks performed. This can range from 10% to 30% of short-term rental income.

3. **Contractual Agreements**: Sign an agreement outlining tasks, responsibilities, and profit sharing to avoid misunderstandings.

b. Advantages and Disadvantages

Advantages:

1. **Collaboration**: Allows sharing of workload and benefiting from the owner's experience and resources.

2. **Easy Entry**: Requires less capital and risk compared to other strategies.

Disadvantages:

1. **Dependency on the Owner**: The quality of collaboration can affect overall success.

2. **Shared Profits**: Profits must be shared, reducing the net margin for the co-host.

4. Innovative Business Models

In addition to traditional strategies, there are innovative business models that allow earning from short-term rentals without owning properties. These include creating management agencies, offering specialized services, and using emerging technologies.

a. Management Agency

Creating a management agency specializing in short-term rentals can be a lucrative way to earn. The agency can offer a full range of management services for property owners, from welcoming guests to maintenance.

1. **Team Building**: Recruit qualified staff to handle various aspects of the business, such as cleaning, maintenance, and guest communication.

2. **Technology and Software**: Use property management software to optimize operations and improve efficiency.

3. **Marketing and Branding**: Create a recognizable brand and promote the agency through various marketing channels to attract owners and guests.

b. Specialized Services

Offering specialized services for short-term rentals can be another source of income. These services may include:

1. **Professional Photography**: Offer photography services to create high-quality images for property listings.

2. **Interior Design**: Provide design consultations to improve the appearance and attractiveness of properties.

3. **Consulting**: Offer advice on optimizing listings, managing reviews, and improving occupancy.

c. Technology and Innovation

Adopting emerging technologies can improve efficiency and create new earning opportunities. Examples include:

1. **Automation**: Use automation systems for booking management, guest communication, and other operations.

2. **Big Data and Analytics**: Use data and analytics to optimize rates, predict demand, and improve marketing strategies.

3. **Proprietary Platforms**: Develop proprietary platforms that connect owners and managers, offering additional services and added value.

5. Partnership Opportunities

Partnerships can be another way to enter the short-term rental market without owning properties. Collaborating with other businesses or industry professionals can provide access to valuable resources and expertise.

a. Types of Partnerships

1. **With Travel Agencies**: Partner with travel agencies to offer accommodation packages to their clients.

2. **With Property Owners**: Establish partnerships with property owners to jointly manage their properties.

3. **With Service Providers**: Collaborate with service providers such as cleaning, maintenance, and key management to offer a complete service to guests.

b. Partnership Benefits

1. **Access to Resources**: Partnerships can provide access to resources, expertise, and networks that can enhance the business.

2. **Risk Sharing**: Sharing risks and responsibilities with partners can reduce the overall burden and improve business sustainability.

Earning from short-term rentals without owning property is possible through a variety of innovative strategies and business models. From managing properties for others to legal subletting, co-hosting, and offering specialized services, there are many opportunities to enter this growing market. The key to success lies in providing excellent service, building strong relationships with owners and guests, and staying updated on industry trends and regulations. With dedication, creativity, and a solid strategy, it is possible to create a profitable and sustainable business in the short-term rental sector without owning properties.

3. Why You Should Start an Airbnb Business Without Owning Property

As mentioned earlier, vacation rentals are experiencing significant growth, driven by changing travel habits and the increasing desire for unique experiences and extended stays. This trend has created new opportunities for those looking to earn in the short-term rental market, even without owning property. Below, we'll explore various ways to enter the short-term rental business and earn with Airbnb without the need to purchase a property.

Advantages of Starting an Airbnb Business Without Owning Property

Lower Investment: Starting to earn with Airbnb without owning a property requires a much lower initial investment, as there's no need for a mortgage or the costs associated with purchasing a property.

Lower Risk: Managing a vacation home requires time, effort, and investment. Being a property manager or offering related services significantly reduces the financial risk compared to buying property.

Greater Manageability: For those seeking a secondary activity, managing properties for others or offering specific services in the short-term rental sector can be much more manageable and accessible than directly managing a vacation home.

How to Start an Airbnb Business Without Owning Property

Become a Property Manager

Many vacation home owners prefer to entrust the management of their properties to professionals known as property managers. This role involves the daily management of properties, ensuring they are always occupied and guests are satisfied.

Property Manager Duties:

1. **Booking Management**: Respond to guest inquiries, manage the booking calendar, and update online listings.

2. **Check-In/Check-Out**: Welcome guests, provide keys and property information, and ensure a smooth check-out process.

3. **Cleaning and Maintenance**: Coordinate cleaning and maintenance services to keep the property in top condition.

4. **Marketing and Promotion**: Create and manage listings on rental platforms, optimizing descriptions and photos to attract more bookings.

How to Start:

1. **Build a Service Portfolio**: Clearly

define the services offered and set competitive prices.

2. **Networking**: Attend real estate events, use social media, and network with property owners.

3. **Join Online Platforms**: Use platforms that connect property managers with property owners, such as Guesty or Vacasa.

4. **Reputation and Reviews**: Build a good reputation through positive reviews from owners and guests.

Offer Marketing, SEO, and Social Media Services

Another way to earn with Airbnb without owning property is to offer marketing and social media management services to vacation home owners. An effective marketing strategy can help properties stand out and attract more guests.

Services Offered:

1. **Search Engine Optimization (SEO)**: Improve the visibility of online listings through SEO techniques.

2. **Social Media Management**: Create and manage social media profiles to promote properties.

3. **Content Marketing**: Write blog posts, create engaging visual content, and develop email marketing campaigns.

How to Start:

1. **Identify the Target Audience**: Understand the target market and develop a tailored marketing plan.

2. **Build a Client Portfolio**: Initially offer services at discounted rates to build a portfolio of positive reviews.

3. **Use Social Platforms**: Promote services offered on platforms like Facebook, LinkedIn, and Instagram.

Start an Airbnb Cleaning Service

Another common way to enter the short-term rental market is to start a cleaning service specialized for vacation homes. Regular cleaning is essential to maintain the high standards required by guests and rental platforms.

Cleaning Service Duties:

1. **Post-Stay Cleaning**: Clean the property between check-outs and new check-ins.

2. **Mid-Stay Cleaning**: Offer cleaning services during longer stays to maintain order and cleanliness.

3. **Standard Property Appearance (SPA)**: Follow specific owner guidelines to ensure the property is always presentable.

How to Start:

1. **Establish Cleaning Contracts**: Sign clear contracts with owners to define expectations and tasks.

2. **Hire Qualified Staff**: Recruit reliable and trained cleaning personnel.

3. **Purchase Equipment and Supplies**: Obtain the necessary equipment and materials to provide high-quality cleaning service.

Offer Upsell Services on Airbnb

Collaborating with Airbnb hosts to offer additional services to guests is another strategy to earn without owning property. These upsell services can enhance the guest experience and increase host earnings.

Upsell Services:

1. **Food Delivery**: Arrange meal or homemade dinner deliveries.

2. **Catering Services**: Offer catering for special events or occasions.

3. **Local Experiences**: Propose activities such as cooking classes, guided tours, or yoga sessions.

4. **Wellness Services**: Offer massages, fitness sessions, or beauty treatments.

How to Start:

1. **Identify Guest Needs**: Understand which additional services would most interest guests.

2. **Establish Local Partnerships**: Collaborate with local providers to offer quality services.

3. **Promote Services**: Use host communication channels to promote upsell services to guests.

Become an Airbnb Co-Host

Co-hosting is a form of collaboration with property owners to help them manage their vacation homes. A co-host can take care of various aspects of management, from guest communication to property maintenance.

Co-Host Duties:

1. **Guest Communication**: Respond to guest inquiries, manage bookings, and provide assistance during their stay.

2. **Property Management**: Ensure the property is clean, well-maintained, and ready for new guests.

3. **Listing Updates**: Keep listings on Airbnb and other platforms up to date.

4. **Review Management**: Monitor and respond to guest reviews to maintain a good online reputation.

How to Start:

1. **Establish a Co-Hosting Contract**: Clearly define the tasks and responsibilities of each party in a written contract.

2. **Build a Portfolio of Owners**: Offer co-hosting services to local owners and build a base of satisfied clients.

3. **Use Management Tools**: Implement tools and software to simplify property management and improve efficiency.

Start a Vacation Rental Management Agency

A more structured option is to start a vacation rental management agency. This type of business can offer a complete range of management services for owners, from online promotion to property maintenance.

Agency Services:

1. **Complete Property Management**: Offer comprehensive management services, including booking management, cleaning, maintenance, and guest reception.

2. **Marketing and Promotion**: Develop marketing strategies to increase the visibility and bookings of properties.

3. **Customer Support**: Provide ongoing support and assistance to both owners and guests.

How to Start:

1. **Build a Team of Experts**: Hire qualified personnel to manage various aspects of the business.

2. **Invest in Technology**: Use property management software to improve operational efficiency.

3. **Promote the Agency**: Create a recognizable brand and use various marketing channels to attract owners and guests.

Partnerships and Collaborations

Partnerships can offer access to resources and expertise that can enhance the business. Collaborating with other companies or professionals in the sector can create beneficial synergies.

Types of Partnerships:

1. **With Travel Agencies**: Collaborate with travel agencies to offer accommodation packages to their clients.

2. **With Property Owners**: Establish partnerships with owners to jointly manage their properties.

3. **With Service Providers**: Collaborate with cleaning, maintenance, and key management service providers to offer a complete service to guests.

Benefits of Partnerships:

1. **Access to Resources**: Partnerships can offer access to resources, expertise, and networks that can enhance the business.

2. **Risk Sharing**: Sharing risks and responsibilities with partners can reduce the overall burden and improve business sustainability.

4. Strategies to Automate and Optimize Your Airbnb Short-Term Rental Business

Managing short-term rentals on platforms like Airbnb can be highly profitable but also requires a significant amount of time and effort. Automating and optimizing various aspects of managing short-term rentals can help you save time, reduce stress, and maximize profits. In this article, we will explore several strategies to automate and optimize your Airbnb short-term rental business.

1. Use Property Management Software (PMS)

Property Management Systems (PMS) are essential tools for automating many of the daily activities associated with managing short-term rentals.

a. Benefits of PMS

1. **Booking Automation**: A PMS can automatically synchronize bookings from various platforms (Airbnb, Booking.com, Vrbo) to avoid overbooking.

2. **Calendar Management**: Facilitates the management of booking calendars, updating them in real-time.

3. **Guest Communication**: Automates responses to guest inquiries and sends pre-defined messages.

4. **Rate Management**: Allows for dynamic pricing based on supply and demand.

b. Popular PMS Examples

1. **Guesty**: A comprehensive platform offering booking management, communication automation, and data analytics.

2. **Hostaway**: Provides tools for booking management, calendar synchronization, and communication automation.

3. **Lodgify**: Allows you to create a

custom website for your property and manage all bookings from one platform.

2. Implement Automated Check-in Systems

Automated check-in systems can significantly reduce the time and effort required to manage guest arrivals.

a. Automated Check-in Solutions

1. **Smart Locks**: Smart locks allow guests to access the property using a temporary code or app, eliminating the need for physical key exchanges.

2. **Lockbox**: A combination safe where keys can be stored, accessible via a code provided to guests.

3. **Key Exchange Services**: Services like KeyNest allow guests to pick up keys from secure collection points located around the

city.

b. Benefits of Automated Check-in

1. **Flexibility**: Guests can check in at any time, enhancing their experience.

2. **Reduced Workload**: Eliminates the need for physical presence during check-in, saving time and effort.

3. **Security**: Smart locks can be easily reprogrammed, enhancing property security.

3. Automate Guest Communication

Automating guest communication can improve their experience and reduce the workload for property managers.

a. Guest Communication Automation Tools

1. **Predefined Messages**: Create templates for common responses (booking confirmation, check-in instructions, check-out reminders).

2. **Chatbots**: Use chatbots to automatically respond to frequently asked guest questions.

3. **Messaging Software**: Tools like iGMS and Smartbnb can automate the sending of messages based on specific events (booking confirmed, one day before check-in, etc.).

b. Benefits of Communication Automation

1. **Time Saving**: Automatically responds to common guest inquiries, reducing the time spent on manual communication.

2. **Consistency**: Ensures that all guests receive clear and consistent information.

3. **Enhanced Guest Experience**: Quick and informative responses improve guest satisfaction.

4. Use Dynamic Pricing Tools

Dynamic pricing allows you to optimize rates based on demand, seasonality, and competition, thereby maximizing profits.

a. Dynamic Pricing Tools

1. **Beyond Pricing**: Analyzes local market data and suggests optimal prices to maximize earnings.

2. **Pricelabs**: Offers dynamic pricing based on various factors, including local events, seasonality, and occupancy.

3. **Wheelhouse**: Provides personalized price recommendations and detailed market analysis.

b. Benefits of Dynamic Pricing

1. **Profit Optimization**: Adjusts prices in

real-time to maximize revenue.

2. **Competitiveness**: Keeps prices competitive relative to other accommodations in the area.

3. **Reduced Manual Work**: Automates price adjustments, saving time spent monitoring and manually updating rates.

5. Automate Cleaning and Maintenance

Automating cleaning and maintenance services can ensure that the property is always ready for new guests without constant involvement.

a. Cleaning and Maintenance Automation Tools

1. **TurnoverBnB**: Automatically synchronizes bookings with the cleaning schedule and sends notifications to cleaners.

2. **Properly**: Allows you to create visual checklists for cleaning tasks and monitor the quality of work via photos.

3. **RoomChecking**: Coordinates cleaning and maintenance tasks, facilitating communication between managers and staff.

b. Benefits of Cleaning Automation

1. **Efficiency**: Automatically schedules cleaning services based on bookings, ensuring the property is always clean and ready for new guests.

2. **Quality**: Improves service quality through detailed checklists and photo verification.

3. **Time Saving**: Reduces time spent manually coordinating cleaning and maintenance services.

6. Implement Feedback and Review Systems

Automating feedback and review collection can help maintain a high level of guest satisfaction and improve your property's online reputation.

a. Feedback and Review Tools

1. **GuestTalk**: Automates the process of requesting feedback from guests after their stay and manages online reviews.

2. **TrustYou**: Analyzes guest reviews and provides valuable insights for improvement.

3. **ReviewPro**: Collects reviews from various platforms and offers detailed analysis to identify areas for improvement.

b. Benefits of Feedback Automation

1. **Immediate Feedback**: Collects feedback in real-time, allowing you to quickly address any issues.

2. **Continuous Improvement**: Provides data and insights to continuously improve the guest experience.

3. **Online Reputation**: Helps maintain a good online reputation through proactive review management.

7. Optimize Your Online Presence

A strong online presence is essential to attract more guests and increase bookings. Optimizing your Airbnb listing and other platforms can make a significant difference.

a. Optimization Strategies

1. **High-Quality Photos**: Invest in professional photography to showcase your property at its best.

2. **Detailed Descriptions**: Write complete and accurate descriptions highlighting the property's strengths.

3. **SEO for Airbnb**: Use relevant keywords in descriptions and titles to improve the visibility of your listing in search results.

4. **Positive Reviews**: Encourage satisfied guests to leave positive reviews to improve your listing's ranking.

b. Optimization Tools

1. **AirGMS**: Automates listing management and optimizes visibility across various platforms.

2. **Rankbreeze**: Analyzes your listing's ranking and suggests improvements to boost visibility.

3. **Hostfully**: Provides digital guides to enhance the guest experience and earn better reviews.

Automating and optimizing the management of short-term rentals on Airbnb can transform a complex and time-consuming process into a more efficient and profitable operation. By using property management software, automated check-in systems, communication tools, dynamic pricing, automated cleaning services, feedback systems, and optimizing your online presence, you can improve operational efficiency, increase guest satisfaction, and maximize profits. With the right strategy and tools, you can manage your short-term rental business more effectively and achieve better results.

5. How to Become a SuperHost and Maximize Your Profits in Short-Term Rentals

Becoming a SuperHost on Airbnb not only enhances the visibility of your property but also increases the trust of potential guests, leading to more bookings and consequently, higher profits. The SuperHost program rewards top hosts who provide exceptional guest experiences. In this guide, we will explore strategies to become a SuperHost and maximize your earnings in short-term rentals.

1. Meet the Basic SuperHost Requirements

Airbnb evaluates SuperHosts quarterly based on specific criteria. Here are the key requirements:

1. **Response Rate of 90% or Higher**: Respond promptly to guest inquiries and

messages.

2. **At Least 10 Stays or 3 Bookings for 100 Nights**: Host at least 10 stays or 3 bookings for a total of 100 nights in a year.

3. **Cancellation Rate Below 1%**: Avoid cancellations unless due to exceptional circumstances.

4. **Average Rating of 4.8 or Higher**: Maintain a high average rating by ensuring guests have positive experiences.

2. Provide Excellent Customer Service

Exceptional customer service is crucial for obtaining positive reviews and becoming a SuperHost.

a. Prompt and Clear Communication

1. **Timely Responses**: Reply to messages within an hour if possible. Use Airbnb app

notifications to stay on top of inquiries.

2. **Predefined Messages**: Use predefined messages to quickly respond to common questions.

3. **Clarity and Detail**: Provide clear and detailed information about the property, including check-in procedures, house rules, and local attractions.

b. Warm Welcome

1. **Personalized Greeting**: Offer a personalized welcome message and perhaps a small welcome gift.

2. **House Guide**: Provide a detailed house guide with information about appliances, Wi-Fi, and local recommendations.

3. **Availability**: Be available for any questions or issues that arise during the stay.

c. Review Management

1. **Request Feedback**: Encourage guests to leave a review, explaining its importance to you.

2. **Respond to Reviews**: Politely respond to all reviews, especially negative ones, showing that you take feedback seriously and are willing to improve.

3. Ensure Impeccable Accommodation

Cleanliness and comfort are essential for receiving positive reviews.

a. Cleanliness

1. **High Standards**: Maintain the property in a clean and orderly state, following strict cleaning standards.

2. **Professional Cleaning**: Consider hiring a professional cleaning service to ensure

everything is perfect.

3. **Quality Control**: Conduct checks after each cleaning to ensure everything is in order.

b. Comfort and Amenities

1. **Comfortable Beds**: Invest in high-quality beds and linens.

2. **Complete Amenities**: Provide all necessary amenities, such as towels, toiletries, kitchen utensils, and working appliances.

3. **Extra Touches**: Offer extras like coffee, tea, snacks, and local products to make guests feel pampered.

c. Maintenance

1. **Regular Maintenance**: Conduct regular checks to identify and address any maintenance issues.

2. **Quick Resolution**: Quickly resolve any

problems reported by guests, such as appliance failures or plumbing issues.

4. Optimize Your Listing

An optimized listing attracts more bookings and improves your position in search results.

a. High-Quality Photographs

1. **Professional Photos**: Invest in professional photography to showcase your property at its best.

2. **Natural Lighting**: Ensure photos are well-lit and taken in natural light.

3. **Detailed Shots**: Show all areas of the property, including details that might interest guests, like the kitchen, bathroom, and common areas.

b. Accurate and Engaging Descriptions

1. **Catchy Title**: Use a title that grabs attention and describes the uniqueness of your property.

2. **Detailed Description**: Provide a complete and detailed description of the property, including amenities and nearby attractions.

3. **Clear House Rules**: List house rules clearly to avoid misunderstandings with guests.

c. Competitive Pricing

1. **Market Research**: Analyze prices of similar properties in your area to set competitive rates.

2. **Dynamic Pricing**: Use dynamic pricing tools to adjust rates based on demand and seasonality.

3. **Special Offers**: Offer discounts for longer stays or special promotions to attract more guests.

5. Offer Unique Experiences

Guests seek memorable experiences. Offering something unique can make a significant difference.

a. Local Experiences

1. **Tours and Activities**: Collaborate with local providers to offer tours, activities, and unique experiences to guests.

2. **Local Guides**: Provide local guides with recommendations for restaurants, attractions, and activities.

3. **Special Events**: Organize special events like wine tastings or cooking classes to enrich the guest experience.

b. Personalized Stay

1. **Guest Preferences**: Ask guests for their

preferences before arrival and try to accommodate them (e.g., pillow type, preferred drinks).

2. **Extra Services**: Offer extra services like airport transfers, bike rentals, or wellness packages.

3. **Attention to Detail**: Small touches like fresh flowers, a welcome note, or a selection of books and games can make a big difference.

6. Monitor and Adapt to Reviews

Reviews are an important source of feedback and can help you continually improve your offering.

a. Review Analysis

1. **Positive Feedback**: Identify what guests like and continue to offer those aspects.

2. **Negative Feedback**: Analyze negative reviews to identify areas for improvement.

3. **Trends**: Look for trends in feedback to understand what you can improve in the long term.

b. Adaptation and Improvement

1. **Immediate Action**: Immediately address any issues reported by guests.

2. **Regular Updates**: Make regular updates to the property and services offered based on feedback received.

3. **Open Communication**: Maintain open communication with guests to understand their needs and continuously improve.

Becoming a SuperHost on Airbnb requires dedication, attention to detail, and a constant commitment to improving the guest experience. By following these strategies, you can achieve SuperHost status and maximize your profits in short-term rentals. Offering exceptional service, maintaining impeccable accommodation, optimizing your listing, and listening to guest feedback will help you stand out in the market and attract more bookings, thereby increasing your earnings.

6. Managing Bookings and Check-in/Check-out in Short-Term Rentals

Efficient management of bookings and check-in/check-out processes is crucial for ensuring a positive guest experience and optimizing operations for property managers in short-term rentals. This involves a range of activities from handling bookings to preparing properties for guest arrivals and coordinating operations during the stay and check-out. We will explore each phase of this process in detail, highlighting common challenges and best practices.

1. Booking and Calendar Management

Booking management begins with listing properties on short-term rental platforms like Airbnb, Booking.com, VRBO, and others. Property managers must keep availability and pricing calendars updated across all platforms to avoid overlaps and ensure efficient capacity management.

Booking Process:

- **Property Listing:** Detailed property descriptions with photos, amenities information, and house rules.

- **Calendar Synchronization:** Using property management software (PMS) to automatically update calendars across all platforms.

- **Cancellation Policies:** Clear definition of cancellation policies to reduce uncertainty for guests and protect managers' earnings.

Common Challenges:

- **Overbooking:** A significant risk if calendars are not properly synchronized.

- **Rate Management:** Adjusting prices based on demand and supply.

Best Practices:

- **Automation:** Using advanced PMS tools to automate booking and calendar management.

- **Constant Monitoring:** Regularly checking calendars to avoid overlaps.

2. Property Preparation

Thorough preparation of the property before guest arrival is essential for ensuring a smooth and pleasant stay.

Cleaning and Maintenance Checklist:

- **Professional Cleaning:** Ensuring the property is thoroughly cleaned between guests.

- **Supplies Replenishment:** Checking and replenishing essential supplies like towels, linens, toilet paper, etc.

- **Maintenance:** Regular checks to ensure all facilities are functioning properly.

Personalization:

- **Personalized Welcome:** Leaving a

welcome message or a small gift for guests.

- **House Instructions:** Providing clear instructions on how to use appliances and house rules.

Common Challenges:

- **Limited Turnaround Time:** Minimizing the time between check-out and the next check-in for thorough preparation.

- **Emergency Management:** Being prepared to handle emergencies like water leaks or power outages.

Best Practices:

- **Efficient Scheduling:** Carefully planning the intervals between stays for complete cleaning.

- **Reliable Team:** Collaborating with dependable cleaning and maintenance service providers.

3. Guest Check-in

Check-in is the first physical point of contact between guests and the property, so ensuring a smooth and welcoming process is essential.

Check-in Methods:

- **Self-Check-in:** Providing clear instructions for self-check-in using codes or digital keys.

- **Personal Welcome:** Greeting by a team member to show the property and answer questions.

Communication:

- **Pre-Check-in Communication:** Sending check-in instructions and contact information in advance.

- **24/7 Support:** Offering continuous support to address any guest questions or issues.

Common Challenges:

- **Guest Delays:** Guests may arrive late, complicating time management.

- **Language Barriers:** Effective communication with guests speaking different languages.

Best Practices:

- **Check-in Automation:** Using technologies like digital keys to facilitate self-check-in.

- **Multichannel Communication:** Using instant messaging and other platforms for efficient communication.

4. Management During Stay

Providing continuous support during the guests' stay is essential to ensure adherence to house rules and overall satisfaction.

Guest Support:

- **Communication Channels:** Offering 24/7 communication channels for assistance and support.

- **Quick Response:** Timely response to guest requests to enhance the overall experience.

Property Monitoring:

- **Security:** Monitoring for safety to ensure guest well-being.

- **Rule Compliance:** Ensuring guests adhere to house and neighborhood rules.

Common Challenges:

- **Complaint Management:** Effectively addressing guest complaints to resolve issues.

- **Unexpected Maintenance:** Handling sudden problems like equipment failures or malfunctions.

Best Practices:

- **Guest Feedback:** Collecting guest feedback to continually improve services.

- **Inspection Routine:** Regular inspections to identify and fix issues before they become major.

5. Guest Check-out

Check-out represents the last physical interaction with guests and an opportunity to quickly prepare the property for the next stay.

Check-out Process:

- **Property Verification:** Inspecting the property for any damages or losses.

- **Key Collection:** Retrieving keys or access codes.

Billing and Refunds:

- **Security Deposits:** Returning any security deposits after property verification.

Common Challenges:

- **Check-out Delays:** Guests might delay check-out, affecting preparation time for the next stay.

- **Property Damage:** Managing accidental damages and compensation claims.

Best Practices:

- **Clear Procedures:** Providing clear check-out instructions and key return procedures.

- **Property Evaluation:** Detailed inspections to detect damages and ensure continuous maintenance.

processes in short-term rentals requires detailed planning, advanced technology use, and effective guest communication. Addressing common challenges with best practices helps property managers ensure positive guest experiences and optimize operations. With a well-defined strategy and implementation of innovative solutions, it is possible to create a hospitable environment and efficiently manage properties, enhancing guest satisfaction and maximizing profits.

7. Marketing and Promoting Your Airbnb Listing for Short-Term Rentals

The success of short-term rentals largely depends on the visibility and attractiveness of your listing on platforms like Airbnb. To maximize bookings and ensure a steady flow of guests, it's essential to implement effective marketing strategies and promote your listing strategically. In this document, we will explore best practices and advanced techniques for promoting your Airbnb listing, covering everything from titles and descriptions to photos and pricing strategies.

1. Listing Optimization

Captivating Title:

- **Key Elements:** Include the type of property, location, and distinctive features (e.g., "Apartment in the Heart of Rome with Panoramic View").

Detailed Description:

- **Highlights:** Emphasize the strengths of your property (e.g., view, modern furnishings).

- **Nearby Attractions:** Describe nearby attractions to increase appeal (e.g., "Steps from Piazza di Spagna and Trevi Fountain").

Quality Photos:

- **Lighting:** Use natural light and lamps to highlight spaces.

- **Varied Angles:** Show different perspectives of the property and its best features.

Common Challenges:

- **High Competition:** Effectively positioning your listing among numerous others.

- **Guest Expectations:** Ensuring photos match reality to avoid disappointment.

Best Practices:

- **Professional Photography:** Invest in a professional photographer for high-quality shots.

- **Persuasive Texts:** Use inviting and persuasive language in the description to attract guests.

2. Pricing Strategies

Market Analysis:

- **Competition:** Monitor the prices of similar listings in your area.

- **Local Events:** Adjust prices based on demand during local events or holidays.

Flexible Pricing Policies:

- **Discounts:** Offer discounts for extended stays or last-minute bookings.

- **Seasonal Rates:** Adjust prices based on the season (high/low).

Common Challenges:

- **Revenue Optimization:** Balancing competitive pricing with maximizing earnings.

- **Demand Fluctuations:** Managing variations in demand that affect availability and pricing.

Best Practices:

- **Automated Pricing:** Use dynamic pricing tools to automatically update prices.

- **Guest Feedback:** Consider feedback on pricing to optimize your pricing strategy.

3. Managing Reviews and Feedback

Immediate Responses:

- **Positive Reviews:** Thank guests for positive feedback and share your commitment to continuous improvement.

- **Negative Reviews:** Respond empathetically, offer solutions, and show your willingness to resolve issues.

Encouraging Feedback:

- **Review Requests:** Kindly ask guests to leave a review after their stay.

- **Follow-Up Messages:** Send a follow-up message to gather immediate feedback.

Common Challenges:

- **Expectation Management:** Ensuring guests have realistic expectations before arrival.

- **Influential Reviews:** Addressing negative reviews that can impact your reputation.

Best Practices:

- **Constructive Feedback:** Use feedback to continuously improve your property and guest experience.

- **Consistent Responses:** Respond to all reviews to show commitment and professionalism.

4. Online and Offline Promotion

Social Media:

- **Visual Content:** Share photos and stories of your property on platforms like Instagram and Facebook.

- **Special Offers:** Announce special offers or exclusive discounts to attract new guests.

Local Collaborations:

- **Local Attractions Partnerships:** Offer discounts or packages in collaboration with local restaurants, tours, or attractions.

- **Community Events:** Participate in local events or fairs to promote your property.

Common Challenges:

- **Online Visibility:** Competing with other listings in the same destination.

- **Reaching the Right Audience:** Identifying and effectively reaching your ideal target guests.

Best Practices:

- **Localized SEO:** Use local keywords in your listings and online content to improve visibility.

- **Affiliate Networks:** Collaborate with other local businesses to promote mutual interests.

5. Continuous Monitoring and Optimization

Performance Analysis:

- **Booking Data:** Monitor the number of bookings and occupancy rate.

- **Guest Feedback:** Use guest comments to identify areas for improvement.

Regular Updates:

- **Listing Updates:** Modify photos or descriptions to reflect improvements or updates to the property.

- **Strategy Adjustments:** Adjust pricing and marketing strategies based on performance and feedback.

Common Challenges:

- **Market Dynamics:** Adapting to changes in traveler preferences and travel trends.

- **Increasing Competition:** Maintaining the competitiveness of your listing against new competitors.

Best Practices:

- **Ongoing Education:** Attend seminars or courses to stay updated on industry best practices.

- **Technological Innovation:** Explore new technologies and tools to improve operational efficiency and guest experience.

Effective marketing and promotion of your Airbnb listing are essential for attracting guests and maximizing revenue in short-term rentals. Investing time and energy in creating a well-optimized listing, managing reviews, and promoting both online and offline can make the difference between a successful property and one struggling to attract guests. With a strategic approach and continuous improvement efforts, you can position your property competitively in the short-term rental market, offering memorable experiences to guests and achieving satisfying financial results.

8. Managing Guest Reviews and Feedback in Short-Term Rentals

Effectively managing guest reviews and feedback is crucial for the success of short-term rentals. Guest opinions directly influence your property's reputation and its ability to attract new clients. In this document, we will thoroughly explore how to efficiently handle reviews and feedback, addressing best practices, common challenges, and strategies for continually improving the overall guest experience.

1. Importance of Reviews and Feedback

Impact on Reputation:

- **Guest Decisions:** Reviews influence future guests' booking decisions.

- **Platform Ranking:** Positive reviews can improve your listing's ranking on platforms like Airbnb.

Constructive Feedback:

- **Improvement Opportunities:** Guest feedback provides valuable insights for identifying areas of improvement.

- **Guest Satisfaction:** Addressing reported issues enhances overall guest satisfaction.

Common Challenges:

- **Negative Reviews:** Handling criticism can be difficult but is essential for managing your reputation.

- **Response Time:** Promptly responding to all reviews requires time and attention.

Best Practices:

- **Regular Monitoring:** Regularly check reviews to respond promptly and manage any issues.

- **Interactive Feedback:** Use feedback to implement tangible improvements in your property and services.

2. Strategies for Receiving Positive Reviews

Creating Memorable Experiences:

- **Personal Welcome:** Greet guests with a smile and provide an overview of the property.

- **Cleanliness and Maintenance:** Ensure the property is clean and well-maintained.

Clear Communication:

- **Before the Stay:** Provide detailed check-in instructions and answer guests' preliminary questions.

- **During the Stay:** Offer support and promptly resolve any issues that arise.

Small Courtesies:

- **Personalized Welcome:** A welcome note or small gift can make a big difference.

- **Post-Stay Follow-Up:** Send a thank-you message and ask for feedback immediately after the stay.

Common Challenges:

- **Unmet Expectations:** Guests may have unrealistic expectations that can negatively influence reviews.

- **Cultural Differences:** Consider cultural differences that may affect guest expectations.

Best Practices:

- **Proactive Feedback:** Kindly ask guests to leave a review without being intrusive.

- **Incentives:** Offer a discount or a small incentive to motivate guests to leave a review.

3. Handling Negative Reviews

Empathetic Approach:

- **Timely Response:** Respond to negative reviews within 24-48 hours to show commitment.

- **Empathy and Resolution:** Be empathetic, acknowledge reported issues, and offer a solution or refund if appropriate.

Constructive Responses:

- **Focus on Solutions:** Concentrate on resolving the problem rather than defending yourself.

- **Private Dialogue:** Invite the guest to contact you privately to discuss the issue further.

Positive Impact:

- **Continuous Improvement:** Use negative reviews as growth opportunities to improve services.

- **Reputation:** Effective management of negative reviews can enhance your overall property reputation.

Common Challenges:

- **Unjust Criticism:** Handling negative reviews that do not accurately reflect your property.

- **Emotional Responses:** Avoid emotional or contentious responses that could further damage your reputation.

Best Practices:

- **Support Team:** Involve your support team to address criticism professionally.

- **Root Cause Analysis:** Identify underlying causes of negative reviews to prevent them in the future.

4. Using Feedback to Improve Guest Experience

Trend Analysis:

- **Recurring Issues:** Identify common

problems mentioned in reviews to specifically improve those aspects.

- **Anonymous Feedback:** Use anonymous surveys to gather unfiltered guest feedback.

Implementing Improvements:

- **Prioritization:** Focus on changes that will have the greatest impact on guest experience.

- **Communication with Guests:** Inform guests of changes made in response to their feedback.

Measuring Results:

- **Post-Implementation Reviews:** Monitor if the changes have had a positive impact on reviews and guest satisfaction.

- **Continuous Adaptation:** Keep collecting and adapting improvement strategies based on feedback received.

Common Challenges:

- **Operational Limits:** Limited resources may hinder the quick implementation of changes.

- **Contradictory Feedback:** Receiving conflicting feedback that makes it difficult to identify corrective actions.

Best Practices:

- **Team Involvement:** Engage your team in reviewing and implementing changes.

- **Feedback as Opportunity:** Turn all feedback, positive or negative, into opportunities for continuous improvement.

5. Advanced Review Management Strategies

Process Automation:

- **Predefined Responses:** Use response templates to speed up review management.

- **Management Software:** Invest in review management software to efficiently monitor and respond.

Sentiment Analysis:

- **Analysis Tools:** Use sentiment analysis tools to understand the tone and sentiment of reviews.

- **Personalized Responses:** Tailor responses based on the specific tone and content of the review.

Collaboration with Satisfied Guests:

- **Brand Ambassadors:** Encourage satisfied guests to share their experiences on social media or with friends and family.

Common Challenges:

- **Cost and Implementation:** Implementing advanced solutions can be costly and time-consuming.

- **Privacy and Security:** Ensure guest data is protected during the review management process.

Best Practices:

- **Continuous Training:** Ensure your team is trained on best practices for review management.

- **Feedback as Innovation Driver:** Use feedback as a guide to innovate and continually improve the guest experience.

Effective management of guest reviews and feedback is fundamental for the success and growth of short-term rentals. Investing time and resources in review management can enhance your property's reputation, attract confident guests, and improve the overall guest experience. With a strategic approach that includes active listening, empathetic responses, and implementing improvements based on received feedback, you can competitively position your property in the short-term rental market and ensure a steady flow of bookings.

9. Problem Resolution and Emergency Management in Short-Term Rentals

In the world of short-term rentals, the ability to promptly handle problems and emergencies is crucial for ensuring guest safety, protecting property, and maintaining a positive reputation. This document focuses on the importance of preparation, response strategies, and best practices for dealing with critical situations in short-term rental services.

1. Preventive Preparation

Risk Assessment:

- **Identifying Potential Issues:** First and foremost, it is essential to conduct a detailed risk assessment. This includes inspecting the property's facilities and infrastructure to identify any weak points such as old pipes or non-compliant electrical systems. Additionally, consider external risks such as natural disasters or security issues in the area.

Emergency Planning:

- **Clear Procedures:** Establish clear and detailed procedures for handling emergency situations. These procedures should cover a wide range of scenarios, including fires, evacuations, road accidents, intrusions, and structural damage.

Staff Training:

- **Roles and Responsibilities:** Assign specific roles and responsibilities to staff and collaborators involved in emergency management. Ensure all personnel are regularly trained on these procedures and know how to act in case of an emergency.

Communication and Emergency Contacts:

- **Contact List:** Maintain an up-to-date list of emergency contacts, including service providers (such as plumbers and electricians), law enforcement, medical and emergency services, as well as the main contact for guests.

2. Managing Common Emergencies

Water Leaks and Plumbing Issues:

- **Immediate Actions:** In case of water leaks or other plumbing problems, immediately shut off the water supply and call a professional plumber. Provide guests with clear instructions on how to mitigate the damage and ensure their safety.

Power Outages and Electrical Issues:

- **Checking Fuses and Breakers:** In case of power outages, check the fuses and breakers before contacting the local electricity provider. Provide guests with flashlights and explain how to safely access emergency exits.

Fires:

- **Evacuation Plans:** Every property should have a detailed evacuation plan visible to all guests. Train your staff and guests on how to act in case of fire, including the placement of fire extinguishers and the use of emergency stairs.

Intrusions and Personal Security:

- **Security Systems:** Invest in adequate security systems such as surveillance cameras and intrusion alarms. Ensure guests are aware of who to contact in case of an emergency and provide instructions for locking doors and windows.

3. Resolving Common Problems

Technical Assistance and Maintenance:

- **Prompt Response:** Respond quickly to guests' requests for technical assistance and maintenance. Keep a detailed log of requests and actions taken to resolve problems.

Cleaning and Sanitation Issues:

- **High Standards:** Ensure your property is cleaned and sanitized to high standards before each guest's arrival. Respond promptly to any complaints regarding cleanliness and offer quick solutions.

Lack of Essential Services:

- **Alternative Planning:** In case of interruptions in essential services like hot water or heating, provide alternative solutions or compensations to guests for the inconvenience caused.

4. Best Practices in Emergency Management

Open and Clear Communication:

- **Communication Channels:** Offer multiple communication channels for guests to reach you easily in case of an emergency. Use instant messaging apps, email, and dedicated phone lines.

Post-Emergency Feedback:

- **Experience Evaluation:** Ask guests to provide feedback on how the emergency was handled once the situation is resolved. Use this information to improve your procedures and response in the future.

Adequate Insurance:

- **Insurance Coverage:** Ensure your property is adequately insured against accidental damage, liability, and other potential risks associated with short-term rentals.

5. Continuous Monitoring and Updating

Procedure Review:

- **Regular Meetings:** Hold regular meetings with your team to review and update emergency procedures based on feedback, past incidents, or changes in the property structure.

Guest Feedback:

- **Review Analysis:** Monitor guest reviews carefully to identify any trends or recurring issues that require immediate attention.

Ongoing Training:

- **Staff Training:** Ensure all staff and collaborators are regularly trained on emergency procedures and problem management.

Problem resolution and emergency management in short-term rentals require detailed preparation, quick response, and effective communication. Investing in preventive preparation, staff training, and the implementation of clear procedures can make the difference between effectively managing critical situations and risking damage to your property's reputation. With a well-defined strategy and proper preparation, you can ensure guest safety, property protection, and maintain a high standard of service, contributing to the long-term success of your short-term rental business.

10. Useful Tips for Successfully Managing Short-Term Rentals

Managing a property for short-term rentals requires a strategic approach and attention to detail to ensure positive guest experiences and maximize financial returns. These 40 tips cover every aspect, from initial preparation to daily management and business growth in short-term rentals.

Initial Preparation

1. **Property Selection:** Choose a property in a desirable location, accessible to transportation and local attractions.

2. **Local Regulations:** Know and comply with local regulations for short-term rentals, including permits and taxes.

3. **Adequate Insurance:** Ensure you have

suitable insurance coverage for short-term rentals, including liability insurance.

4. **Property Preparation:** Prepare your property with attention to detail, ensuring it is clean, well-furnished, and safe for guests.

5. **Clear Documentation:** Draft clear rental agreements outlining house rules, cancellation policies, and other important information for guests.

Guest Planning

6. **Booking Channels:** Use various booking platforms to maximize your property's visibility and reservations.

7. **Competitive Pricing:** Determine a competitive price based on your location, property features, and local demand.

8. **Cancellation Policies:** Offer flexible cancellation policies to attract more bookings and retain guest loyalty.

9. **Smooth Check-in/Check-out:** Arrange a simple and clear check-in and check-out process to ensure a stress-free experience for guests.

10. **Customer Support:** Provide prompt and available customer support to answer questions and resolve issues before and during the stay.

Operational Management

11. **Preventive Maintenance:** Schedule regular maintenance checks for the property, including plumbing, electrical systems, and security.

12. **Professional Cleaning:** Invest in professional cleaning services to ensure the property is always in impeccable condition for each guest.

13. **Basic Supplies:** Ensure your property is well-stocked with essentials like linens, towels, cleaning products, and toiletries.

14. **Pricing Management:** Use dynamic pricing tools to update prices based on demand and market changes.

15. **Security Systems:** Install effective security systems such as intrusion alarms, surveillance cameras, and safes for guest safety.

Guest Experience

16. **Personal Welcome:** Greet guests with a smile and provide them with an overview of

the property and house rules.

17. **Local Guide:** Provide a local guide with information on restaurants, attractions, and transportation to help guests enjoy their stay.

18. **Additional Services:** Offer additional services such as airport transportation, bicycle rentals, or guided tours to enrich the guest experience.

19. **Proactive Communication:** Communicate with guests before, during, and after their stay to answer their questions and ensure they have everything they need.

20. **Feedback and Reviews:** Kindly ask guests to leave reviews and feedback to continuously improve your property and service.

Marketing and Promotion

21. **Quality Photos:** Invest in professional photographs of your property to attract guest attention on booking sites.

22. **Captivating Description:** Write a detailed and persuasive description of your property, highlighting its strengths and unique features.

23. **Local SEO:** Use local keywords and optimize your listing to improve visibility in online searches.

24. **Special Promotions:** Offer discounts or special packages to attract guests during low season or local events.

25. **Social Media:** Use social media to promote your property, share positive reviews, and engage with potential guests.

Review Management

26. **Review Responses:** Respond promptly and professionally to all reviews, both positive and negative, to show commitment and care.

27. **Constructive Feedback:** Use guest feedback to improve services and resolve any reported issues.

28. **Review Incentives:** Offer a discount or small incentive to guests who leave a review after their stay.

29. **Managing Negative Reviews:** Address negative reviews with empathy, offering solutions and demonstrating your commitment to improvement.

30. **Performance Monitoring:** Monitor reviews and ratings to assess your property's

performance and make necessary adjustments.

Finance and Economic Management

31. **Expense Control:** Carefully monitor operating expenses such as utilities, cleaning, and maintenance to ensure economic management of the property.

32. **Revenue Forecasting:** Use historical data and forecasting tools to plan revenue and manage financial expectations.

33. **Taxes and Duties:** Ensure you understand and fulfill tax obligations related to short-term rentals in your jurisdiction.

34. **Clear Accounting:** Maintain accurate accounting of all income and expenses associated with your property.

35. **Tax Planning:** Consult a professional to optimize tax planning and maximize the financial benefits of your business.

Innovation and Adaptation

36. **Technology and Automation:** Use advanced software and technologies to efficiently manage bookings, communications, and daily operations.

37. **Guest Feedback as Innovation Driver:** Use guest feedback to identify new service opportunities and continuously improve the guest experience.

38. **Ongoing Training:** Regularly update your skills and those of your team through training and professional development.

39. **Environmental Sustainability:** Implement sustainable practices such as

recycling, using renewable energy, and eco-friendly products to attract environmentally-conscious guests.

40. **Expansion and Diversification:** Explore opportunities to expand or diversify your business, such as through new properties or strategic partnerships.

Successfully managing a short-term rental property requires a combination of strategic planning, attention to detail, and a constant commitment to service excellence. By implementing these 40 tips, you can enhance the overall guest experience, increase bookings, and build a solid reputation in the short-term rental market. Continue to monitor industry trends, adapt to changes, and seize opportunities to grow and develop your business successfully.

Index

1. Introduction pg.4

2. How to Earn with Short-Term Rentals Without Owning Property pg.15

3. Why You Should Start an Airbnb Business Without Owning Property pg.27

4. Strategies to Automate and Optimize Your Airbnb Short-Term Rental Business pg.40

5. How to Become a SuperHost and Maximize Your Profits in Short-Term Rentals pg.53

6. Managing Bookings and Check-in/Check-out in Short-Term Rentals pg.63

7. Marketing and Promoting Your Airbnb Listing for Short-Term Rentals pg.73

8. Managing Guest Reviews and Feedback in Short-Term Rentals pg.82

9. Problem Resolution and Emergency Management in Short-Term Rentals pg.93

10. Useful Tips for Successfully Managing Short-Term Rentals pg.101

www.ingramcontent.com/pod-product-compliance
Lightning Source LLC
Chambersburg PA
CBHW071937210526
45479CB00002B/720